Passions:

Love Poems and Other Writings

By Gabriela Marie Milton

To C.

"O naked flower of my lips, you lie! I await a thing unknown or perhaps, unaware of the mystery and your cries you give, O lips, the supreme tortured moans of a childhood groping among its reveries to sort out finally its cold precious stones."

Stephane Mallarme

Table of Contents

Poems translated in Italian by Flavio Almerighi............89

Foreword

Gabriela Marie Milton is the type of poet Robert Graves had in mind when he referred to being a poet as a condition – rather than a profession. During my correspondence with Milton, it became clear that the lush scenes and stories in this collection were not invented as much as they were unleashed. They came from a mind always teeming with ideas, anticipating those moments of expression when the stuff of thought finds its form in lines, rhythm, and stanzas.

As Milton said in an interview, "The days in which I cannot write, I have to compartmentalize my brain and my soul, and then bury my fantasies...It's as if I must exorcise my alter ego." Yes, Gabriela Marie Milton is a poet of condition.

Her poetry also takes on a cosmopolitan character, introducing the reader to diverse, sometimes fantastical, spaces. In some of these spaces, I cannot help but see fragments of her life flickering by – of being raised in Europe or of her extensive travels before and after settling in the United States. But in all of this movement, we're greeted by a common theme: the universality and borderlessness of love and passion. This is where her collection truly shines, and this is where her poetry must be experienced – rather than explained.

Brian Geiger,
Editor of Vita Brevis Press

Acknowledgments

I am deeply grateful to Christina Schwarz, the author of the New York Times Bestseller *Drowning Ruth*, for reading the manuscript of my book and for offering me her wonderful insights into my poetry.

I am also thankful to the great Italian poet, Flavio Almerighi, for translating several of my poems – included in this book - into Italian, a language that I love deeply.

Last but not least, I am grateful to you, my dear reader – wherever you are in this world – for your willingness to spend time with my poetry and to walk the roads of passion and fantasy with me.

Welcome to my book, my dear reader. For you, I wrote these poems. For you, I opened the doors of passion, love, and imagination. Look no further. Come with me, and together we will defy mortality.

Gabriela Marie Milton

Love Poems:

The miracle of you

the moon's right-hand
pours soul into my flesh
pigeons' wings bring scents of lilac blooms
the air gets drunk with poetry
statuary women of the water
flaunt their hair

within the loneliness of you
my heart
rotates five equinoxes on a wooden spindle
your eyes pour flesh into my soul
my body germinates the sounds of growing leaves
I wash my hands into the waters of Guadalquivir
in the scented night of those who never sleep
I say
I love you
and in one single breath
our wedding is transformed
in an enraptured death

was it the moon?
was it the morning dew?
perhaps it was the miracle of you

Spring's floral certitude

I can't see you
the spring's floral certitude
showers petals in my eyes
lingers on veils forgotten at the altars
dreams interpret the language of cicadas
somebody plays the violin in the green room
like a flamenco dancer in Seville
I toss and turn inside my soul
your breath scatters on my neck
I stretch my arms to harvest poems
tongues of fire from your eyes
linger on my silky dress
I fall
rose thorns bite my thighs
it smells earth and grass from an old spring
I turn the page
I close my eyes
and I can see you

The hour of sunsets

frontiers of my being
the hour of sunsets has come
with bare hands I drown you in the coldest seas
red lilies burn you in the hidden valley
predatory birds delight in carnal straps
I run barefoot through streets of no return
I knock on doors
a piece of bread
for my entire heart
oh, it's midnight
I step into the land of fantasies that are not mine
I play with dreams like children play with kites
fires taller than the sky burst from my pregnant heart
nocturnal marigolds crawl on my skin like ants
I interrupt the voice of number Pi
from the clouds
I rain on you, my love, the silence of the prophets without tongues
was that a ray of light?
skyscrapers yawn
destinies melt in the taste of coffee and mistrust
coughs of cars
the day confines me to the sick banality of its own land
my hands, aquatic pillars of forgotten fantasies
wait like thieves on corners of the streets
for yet another night

The lonely poetry of night

trees whisper, cries of cloudy skies
inaudible, unseen,
you, Astraea,
you push me on a long-forgotten trail
the ocean, poisoned, green, unsettled
warm tongues, ecstasies of memories un-lived
defiled the innocence of maiden-stars
tears, corridors of sand
you, universe that dreamt us all
the pain of suffocated myths that die
kisses, floating sanctuaries
Astraea,
you who don't know desire
burn the nihilism of flesh
the plight
of souls sold for two pennies in slave markets
inside the lonely poetry of night

Bewitched

perhaps I was bewitched by the North Star
or by a ballad as dateless as my blood
geography of feelings populates unwanted interludes
my eyes, the nests of dewy grass and leaves
emerald eyelashes flaunt
black taffeta chirps between my fingers like piano keys
inside my soul your kisses soar
soft lilac tones like prayers of the youngest nun
perhaps because I read your poetry last night
and cut my soul between a stanza and a strife
perhaps a child played with a kite
a kingdom for a sup
maybe it was the wind
that woke me up

With this ring I promise you

with this ring
I promise you
I will erase the shadows of the slave trade
locked in the heat of samba in the nights of carnival
coins put on the eyes of dead at funerals
-forgotten tickets of the unforgotten underworld- will shine like
stars
with stolen leaves from the old olive tree
I'll wash your temple covered by the sand and blood of the
bullfights
and mend the bones of sugar skulls spread on the Aztec lands
I will return your boat to shore with one single I love you
in dark I will immerse your soul into the waters of Guadalquivir

listen,
when the ocean laments in the purple of sunsets
the orange-yellow striping of green anacondas fades in dust
when phantoms intoxicated by the worlds of purple belladonnas
and of grass
grasp in search of a tomorrow that may never come
I'll draw the road of love on your old navigation maps
the burning of the boats will stop
and moons will drop blueberry honey on your face and palms
with this ring
made from the muscle of my lively heart
I promise I will love you till the end
when you will travel the whole earth
in search of that which is the scent of me

I am the one

I am the voice of your past loves
resounding in your wildest fantasies
dressed in roses at the altar of your dreams
I am the one you've never had
my soul flows from the tears of the Nile
from the hands of children who still beg
through ruins, darkness, and deep pain
through wars which they will never understand
I am the last who will be saved
for I have sinned under the shadow of His cross
when Spanish fountains cry in the sunset
I am the Desdemona who you've never met
today Granada's just the place
in which García Lorca once was killed
I am the feather of a gold macaw bird
and in the city where bells toll
I am the one whose cries you've never heard

Sunday on another latitude

The smell of orange trees blooms in my hair.
Days of magic: a lily and a rose.
A purple sky bites from the imperishable yellow coiled around
your finger.
Dark injured blood taints the possibility of the sunset.
The exertion of a prayer.
The reflection of our faces in a desiccated well.
Sunday on another latitude.

Prayers

whisper,
you who know to whisper
intercessions
(prayers on behalf of others)
songs of love and songs of sorrow
for the sailors from the depths of the tomorrow
sleepy bibles rub their eyes
in the Basilica of San Nicola

whisper,
you who know to whisper
adorations
(homages to blooming flowers)
on Sunday afternoon the air is moist
dressed in irises and sandalwood
the tropic breathes mangoes and strawberries
symphonies crave passions made of sand
on columns signs of the old lovers

and,
when you reach the point of the confession
stop whispering
and look at me
I am your love
your sin, and your redemption
I don't know the past
I don't know the future
I am the last verse of an unknown psalm
and the forever ardor
captured in between your palms

What I want

a tipsy air plays with my dress
golden afternoons fall from my hair
fingers, pillars of the city
point toward the dangers of an angry sea

why are my ships hit by deceptive languor?
what have you done to them to fall in love with you?
I rip my pain
I throw it to the waves
I raise my head
and speak to you

what do I want?

I want to sail to the East Indies
to bathe in essences of coriander and of cinnamon
to meet the founders of the now adulterated cities
exchange my soul for silky fabrics in Jaipur

to walk in temples nested in the banyan trees
to bite the skin of passion fruits in naked nights
to tear my heart and throw it to Lord Vishnu
to soil my hands while healing beggars in the streets

oh, I know…
your love which always looks for me
a kiss forgotten in a drawer
everything one day will wash at sea

and that will be the day in which
fingers, pillars of the city
will turn your love
toward the real me

The secret of a hand fan

I am here.

I am in the breeze that dries the evening's sweat from your chest.

I pray covered by petals of fresh roses.

I can smell you: scents of burning suns, oranges, and battered seas.

Hallucinations of an acoustic guitar. Its body shape melts under your fingers like candy on the tongue of a little girl.

You and me running barefoot on cobblestone streets.

The rim of my red dress torn.

Against cracked walls the same night plays with our dreams over and over again like children play with colored kites.

You didn't think I would come back.

Well, I did.

The secret of a blue hand fan slides on my rosy cheek.

The moon undresses the wings of an angel.

I smile.

Nordic play

an island shimmers on the Nordic sea
your eyes are madness and pale blue
under your fingers the piano
ennobles pain and makes the snow to fall
play the melancholy of winter
white adulterated by a frozen mauve
I'll make the bed and walk in silence
to the place of roses and of cinnamon
don't follow me
remain and play under the blues of winter
the scented mystery of all the women
who never knew
the fires hidden
in the glaciers of your soul

Andalusian Resurrection

open your veins Andalusia
let him drink from your lynx blood
inject the rhythms of the flamenco
under the coldness of his eyes
tattoo his flesh with tiles of azurite
pour the sounds of castanets
into his arms
my fingers swirl
the flesh of ripened olives
covers the old shroud
the flow of blood from the white shirt
has stopped
I hear his voice
there is one cross
and you're my only love
my body arches
oils flame in my hair
a Moorish verse falls from a wall
covering my cries
Andalusia
I kneel among your cacti fed by salt
your wounded lashes
resurrected him
for yet
another night

I'll return

I open my veins in warm waters
each time when you like what I write
the sound of the sands in the darkness
the eyes of the desert are dried
the midnight windows are opened
I jump like a lynx from a cage
dressed in cold winds and in black
barefoot
I land on the yolk of young times

I paid all the bills do not worry
I buried my bracelets by the green wall
white shirts are lined in the closet
this sand tastes like canvas and paint
I sharpen my eyes
my fingers are stretched
from the cosmic tomorrow
I enter tonight

I'll return do not worry
disheveled, loves cry between us
remember the words of the Persian Sibyl
who sold you my soul for three coins?
the time is fluid like rivers
water lilies can bloom in the sand

Marry Me

Midnight suspends itself on a rock wall
the Hands of Fatima knit shades of blue over the valley
sounds, chirps of migratory birds
flutter of old keys hidden in lonely drawers
run with me and let's get married
the forest speaks
dark silhouettes of that which may not be
antediluvian, the fingers of all virtues and desires
walk barefoot in my grandmother's finest shawls

braid my hair with smells of lavender and roses
grow green leaves on skins of tapestries
the moon sets altars among trees
frantic crickets play the violins of dusk
steel a star and set it on my finger
scents of berries and of pines sigh promises of love
bewitched, the trees shed their golden sap at our feet
souls, the confluence of unknown rivers
wounds inside the labyrinths of mind

I harvest pain and joy from prophesies and sands
I make the valley grow the heaviest of wheat
I let those who are not,
to be
a nightshirt lies on a deceptive bed of flowers
with naked hands pick all my reveries
the night is pregnant with starscapes
marry me!

Those roses which die in the winter

those roses which die in the winter
played the piano last night
a whirlpool of notes and of poems
inscribed on a wall painted in blue
caged in your dreams I still struggle
like birds drowned in water and mud
I cover the world with my fingers
I haunt the unspoken in dark
those roses which died before blooming
this love which will end in a tomb

Fires

fires burn rocks in the mountains
fountains in the parks burn our hearts
I dip my hands into the seven parallels of love
I spin the planetary souls on both my arms
a bird pulls at its feathers in the mirror
the wilderness of autumn
puts on its lipstick

insanity throws stones into a garbage can
exiled from the imagination of Seville
Don Juan lures empty frames inside a bar
your heart meanders among marble stars
scents of flowers, heavy chains
poetry burns our lips
lonely scavengers of night
you and I

Samos, perhaps Crete

on the barren shore
you play your mandolin
I conjugate "to leave" in the voice of trees
the air reverberates expressions of old gods
the space changes its mind
maybe it is Samos, perhaps it is just Crete
traces of death, glimpses of the future
your thoughts are cut in marble
scratches turn to yellow
delineations, conquerors of islands
the shore melts in the waters
your eyes tell prophesies
the time changes its mind
perhaps it was just Samos, maybe it was Crete
the dying mandolin, the smell of ripened olives
an unmade wooden bed
solemnity, delirium
the names of I,
You
We

At the edge of winter

at the edge of winter
bridal chambers cry
roasted chestnuts crack
in the frigid streets
days inside my soul
come and go like ships
broken hearts lament
right at my front door
did I leave you there?

see,
I can't remember
what I've done with you
at the edge of winter
a tree is sick with flu

Luscious

tulips shed their virgin looks
palm trees bend
birds rotate the purple of the clouds
dolphins
luscious skin on luscious skin
I pack an ocean
two flowers
and a dream

The healing asphodel

pain
thunderstorms
swing the windows of the *Hôpital de la Charité*
the trees drop on the roof their liquid green
fomented venom from some salivary glands
awakened phantoms of short lives
long necks are not in fashion anymore
nor are the elongated nudes
depravity
the hand that takes
bites from the one that gives
a drop of vitriol stains my white dress
I hurt
I look into the eyes of a reclining nude
on my décolleté
affixed
a healing asphodel

Hidden

hidden
inside the majesty of time
among the gestures of demoted lovers
winds are pushing boats to shore
letters written now by others
inside the folds of our time
the spleen of forests that are cut
child brides are crying terrified
skin is showing purple marks
a Stradivarius which was never made
plays the tunes of your own mind
hidden
inside the letters of your name
the dormancy of our love

Waltz

I waltz into an empty ballroom
yesterday the ghost of Maja haunted Goya in the streets
hungry demons haunted you
effervescence, the molecules of those who'll never be,
a door gets slammed
a key gets turned
the breath of earth is choked
initiation
my hair gets caught deep in the coldness of the stars
my fingers trace a rainbow in the inky sky
I buried our wedding bands
inside the mist of that which never is
I snow on you white flowers from the one forbidden tree
I jump like a wild lynx
I look for prey
you make pianos sneeze old rhapsodies
stop
it is too late to understand
who's me

Autumn Neuroses

your eyes are young
my breath is heavy
sunflowers vanish in the frost
the tea is boiling
and the cat is purring
it's autumn in the northern hemisphere
while summer comes on Rio de la Plata
I knew a poet who once said
I want to die unknown on Rio de la Plata
his eyes were old
his arms were strong
I ran to you into the northern hemisphere
and autumn came
to bury me in its neuroses' mold
your body's warm
my body's cold
the room is quiet like a tomb
a nun is kneeling in the street
it's autumn in the northern hemisphere
while summer comes on Rio de la Plata

The forgetfulness of summer

On my left mountains of passion lost in lunar light.
On my right poetry.
An African violet beats her eyelashes.
Spanish moss lingers on the waters of the Bayou.
The smell of fresh cocoa penetrates my nostrils.
Old wounds crawl on my skin; columns of ants searching for
honeydew on a tropical tree.
The forgetfulness of summer.
The silence of a blue lagoon.
You.

Children of the first Amen

we were young when our autumn
came to burn leaves in the park
drunk with iambic pentameters
you called me Beatrice by the old fountain
we floated high in the veined sky
in the clouds we lit a candle
with threads of love we sewed our lips
children of the first Amen
we did not see the rain was coming
like heavy fruits forgotten by a harvester on trees
we fell on the same bench right by the fountain
the autumn burned us
and gale winds
blew our ashes to nowhere

Amour (Never sinned)

amour
your eyes are apple green
my eyes are forged in fire
tears of joy hold hands
the sky is blue
the air is pure
the music blooms
we didn't sleep
yet why does this morning feel
like we have never sinned?
amour

Confession

endless
nights of passion
mornings of confession
between the ebb and flow
an unreachable love
sounds of cellos
contradict themselves
the silent witness
a pale moon
perhaps I dreamed you

Sounds of flutes

listen to the horses gallop in the water
in the midst of autumn
axes of gold passion
intersect cold laughter
chestnuts crack the time
heaving their fruits
bake my lips with love
born from sounds of flutes

Souls

I had to go through your soul
to get to mine
once in mine
I wish
I would have stayed in yours
boats
memories of that port where demons haunted you
empty chests
our hearts taken out every evening
mornings
pumping despair and agony
no blood left
between your soul and mine
an autumn naked sky

Dreams of me

tonight
I will come
to your room
from the ocean of a forgotten autumn
you will be asleep
on the left side of the bed
in the morning
your chest will smell salt
a cardinal will trill
dreams of me

Ropes of destiny

you're looking at the vial
I'm looking at the dagger
neither of us
worthy of redemption
tale of the Verona lovers
the die is cast
vain efforts to escape each other end nowhere
love
erotic pollen
settles between us
it rips my heart apart
it makes your heart bit faster
ropes of destiny
tie us
forever

Syllogism of lust

I follow you onto old streets
hermetic sealers, principles of dark
alchemy, the name of you and me
windows of the courtesans from Syracuse
on which some neophytes waste their time
a boat which never leaves the shore
my body, syllogism of lust
fertility of the flatlands
disoriented rivers confluent on maps
the seventh circle turns into the eighth
don't stop
people like money, they don't like art
the wisdom of old sages hidden in plain sight
I wasn't Beatrice
I should have been
forgive me father, for I've sinned
inside the gnostic bridal chamber
I fell in love with him

Love in blue and black

my love,
I speak to you through centuries of pain
trees spin barren branches in the air
when loneliness rains on blue hills
I crush my heart
so yours can still beat
listen
ocean waves embrace the moon's pale chest
instead of tears
I shed naked pearls
to wash the effigy of your acoustic agony
and mend the painful scratches from your skin
with my imaginary fingers
in blue and black the time I bend
and no matter who I am
a human or a spirit
I swear to you
I'll love you till the end

Before you came: the day of the fallen saints

you do not know
how many countries I have traveled
how many marvels I have shown myself
the names of the dead souls I've resurrected
my victims' kisses buried in a pink conch shell
inside the whispers of the messianic Nazareth
He who knew of His own crucifixion
picked up my tears
broke the bread
so I could lock the memory of my first kiss
inside the rocks of the eternal Spanish Steps
and walk again through fields of roses and lavender
into gestating dreams of no constraints

yet see,
all that happened
before the day you came into my life
the day when all the fallen saints
mysteriously
were set free

Hunter

the destiny that calls me
will have to wait tonight
for I am hunting Judas
and I am hunting Brutus
blood boils in my veins
I'm sharpening my arrows
I strangulate the time
I coil around your thoughts
hunter of desires
the Mount of Olives cries
my hands are fighting lions
the mystery of me
is bursting into fires

Out to sea

tonight
I will sleep
on your right shoulder
wings of birds
will cover us
in the morning
the breeze will blow us
out to sea
poems
buried in the waves

Triolets

a violet sunset laments in the city
saps of triolets flow on my neck
ah, Granada
I stretch inside your memory
like felines on grasslands
a lily cries
my bracelets dangle
the eyes of candles flicker in your Spanish nights

fingers of lascivious desires
steal from my neck the saps of triolets
Granada
play your magical guitars
unleash the beauty hidden in your walls
the frenzy of the flesh which dies
into the ardent gestures of your dance
under La Puerta de Elvira
yesterday two lovers met
and I,
I wait in tears
for the love
which knows the mysteries of triolets

Shiver

A full moon weeps cold fragrant oil on my face.
Shiver.
The cicadas' song penetrates the membranes of the space.
On one of my arms a purple mark sighs and then falls asleep.
Looking for prey a snake's tongue splits the time in two.
I feel the bite.
You.

Fated Cravings

I was born under the salty light of underwater stars
when autumn leaves were burning
the neurotic passions of forgotten lovers
three fates surrounded my rosewood cradle
the Spinner threaded all my life from purple silk
her fingers soft
her lips a nest of loving birds
the Allotter gave me the sensuality of painted nudes
the interruption of the sanctity of times when church bells toll
the Inevitable fated me with your aquatic soul
inside the smell of the fresh grass and dreams
I've learned to crave for your dark eyes
liked wisdom craves for ancient scrolls

Lovers without love

you, quest of lovers without love
your unrelenting islands beaten by the wind-blown sand
the sea
extends its waves beyond the singularity of night
the silk of clouds is looking for the sky
scales of reeds chime songs,
cries of those whose loves have sunk

I bathe in the aromatic rose of the moonlight
the night bathes in the foam of the blue waters
a bed sighs
the silhouettes of three carnations gossip on the floor
alienation
empty hearts expecting to be slaughtered

the sand receives me
in the distance a mast decides to flicker
the quest of lovers without love
on a wicker chair
a lonely glove

No one's world

I can hear the rifle firing
I'm trying not to think
I'm counting empty chairs in a small bar
the polish on my nails is red
my lipstick must be red
I don't have a mirror
the rifle fires again
I can hear the screams of children
I can hear the screams of brides
it smells anesthetic
death sounds like newborns

bartenders polish glasses
trying to remember where exactly
they belong…

and in no one's world
lamentations tear at my soul
the hunger games are heating up
and your coffee's getting cold

Founders of love

I patch your wounds
you kiss my hands
I cry
you laugh
the Spinner threads our life
the Archer shoots the moon
sanctified
our house grows in trees
your hands and mine
founders of love
a church bell tolls
I steer the boat
you raise the sail
serenities of underwater stars
another brick
another tear
another year

Leaves of poetry

Fathoms of your kisses float on my fingers.
Water lilies sleep on green lips of hidden lakes.
Leaves of poetry murmur in a willow tree.
Ripped apart by the gallop of an Arabian horse the night bleeds.
Sand and blood. Memories of the forgotten breath of our Sahara:
the Sahara in which fate played games.
Spaces, times, light crawl upon each other like flapping fish in a
net.
The enigma of "to be."
The simplicity of me.

The day that never comes

the sea throws fishing nets into the sky
the blood of stars drops on a lonely shore
acoustic
ships fantasize under the reddish voice of night
fingers of the truth pulsate inside the wombs of underwater weeds
I comb my hair with dreams of roses and of salt
you smoke cigars within the loneliness of banyan parks
and in our island where all Mondays dress in black
our Tuesdays lock the saints in cages built from tentacles of mud
synapses snap
confused, the ships engage in fratricide,
mercenaries, the new gods, turn statues made of marble into dust
on Sundays, intoxicated by the smell of oleanders, we make love
hallucinations separate the blood of stars from sand
and by the sea which throws its fishing nets into the sky
we wait for the true day
the day that never comes

I am your soul

look for me my love
my body shines like lightening
striking down from Mount Olympus
I'm the tremble of each tear
which poor hungry children shed
I'm the prayer of the lonely
the garden where the virgins blush
the mystic bite of occult ecstasies
I'm hidden in the Sistine Chapel
in haunted graveyards at midnight
I'm bursting from the keys of the piano
which plays alone Beethoven's 5th

now
call for God
breathe me in
I am your soul

Hellenistic reverie

caressed together by the waters of Corinth
inside the darkest forests chasing statuary nymphs
the decadence of Hellenistic love
blissfully raining laughter from above

"the condo of the virgin" sitting empty
the goddess long dissolved into the néant
you softly reading Hebrew texts in Greek
the painful comedy of life on sale this week

Effigy of loss

The ocean caught a glimpse of our past: love roots starting and
ending in us.
In the distance, a white sail: the giant wing of a wounded albatross.
Red, blue, yellow giving to gold: the vastness of dead sands.
An insidious wave disturbed the effigy of loss.
You.

Memories

Meadows where trees sleep, and rivers stretch like cats.
Fairies dance tarantella in the air.
Your purple lips reflect the shadows of the women you will love.
Memories.
Your eyes as thirsty as the surface of the moon.
Sandy dunes.

Summer fantasy

my eyes are water wells
mirroring your body
into a time which shrinks
my lips shine on stained glass
windows to the sea
a virgin violin
faints into your lap
sick with jealousy
the summer hangs in trees
seduction
fantasy

Delusion

lurking at the margins of your love
my mind
does not expand and does not shrink
delusion
the lake reflects the light of a dead star
a seagull heaves upward
an aching call
dissonance
the cosmic Adam does not care
that I was set on his left side

Viking Boats

I will cover
your soul with mine
a white cloak
covering the earth
nobody will hear
your frightened cries
you will heal

then
I would disappear
at sea
like mortuary
Viking boats

Wooden bed

I know some fields
in which the flesh of poppies smiles
when blonde sunsets play classical guitars
I know the coffee shop in which you stop
the gypsy lady who foretold our luck

listen,
inside the shadows of the night of eucalyptus
winds unbraid their fragrant hair
a moon serves wine in crystal glasses
inside the mirrors blue souls dance in pairs

I have to go
I can't write more
send my kisses to the ocean's waves
don't sell the wooden bed in which we first made love
the dress embroidered by my mother's hands
save the letters that my father wrote before he died
I'm rushing
guards are coming
my wrists will be soon stamped

yours forever,
from a concentration camp

Aquatic Sorcery

Liquid shoulders touched by wings of albatrosses shiver.
The occult aroma of the volcano goddess cries.
A lily and a rose light candles in the dark.
My pregnant soul invokes my ancestors.
Ecstasy encroaches its eight hands around your naked chest.
A lonely pearl looks for its shell.
Tears shed in silence.
Aquatic sorcery of immortal dreams.

Amour

amour
your secret hides inside my name
inside the splendor of the night in which you didn't say a word
feathers of macaw birds trace music sheets
the rays of sun stretch on the pebble beach
a fragrant song delights itself on my red lips
I rest my head on your left shoulder
into the lands of spices waiting to be born
we fall
some carnal dreams howl on the corridor
who cares?
I locked the door!
this morning we can die
we won't tell a soul
and never ask for more
amour

You

you
cradle filled with lava
eating from veined skies
voice which breaks through trees
rocking birds of night
dangling long earrings
ferment in your blood
yesterday
tomorrow
coins which make no sense
you
who marked your name
in silence
on my chest

Trap me

trap me
in the rhythms of the Flamenco
whose sounds invade the nights of Southern Spain
to breathe the notes of the guitars which play
and fill the lustrous eyes with burning pain

trap me
in the Florence of my dreams
to walk with Leonardo in its streets
to cry with the Madonna and to verse in Greek
when the last word of Christ forever speaks

trap me
in a Hindu monastery
in splendid nights my sufferings unpacked
and in the shadow of Mandala
give me the power never to come back

Scents of flowers and of salt

pain is dripping from guitars
into sunsets with no end
pigeons guide ships lost at sea
tears drop from plumy skies
love is blowing in the wind
scents of flowers and of salt

listen
to the night of oleanders
to the magic of the key which turns
take me to the kiss of no return
when the sky is turning blue
and we're centuries apart
let me kneel in front of you

Heritage of the unknown

I kneel
you pray
a bird rises from the ashes
inside my soul
the desperation of the boats which never leave the shore
tolls the waves like a church bell
the moon gets pregnant with desires
aquatic flowers creep on my right arm
the poet of the city long forgotten
loneliness hangs on the streets
the myth of the Verona lovers worn
within the cycles of the moon
the heritage of the unknown
tries desperately
to be born

Sea Snake

One hundred degrees Fahrenheit in the shade.
The scent of you and that of the salty ocean.
Sand in your hair.
Your wet shirt coiled at my feet.
Inside the echoes of a pink conch, my love for you tosses like a
newborn in a crib.
A paddle-like tail raises from the water; a sea snake.
Your green eyes devour me.
Why is there always a snake inside the core of our myths?

Did you say you love me?

I breathe in an unfamiliar rhythm.
The sun metamorphoses into a golden liquid.
Glittering rivers inundate the sky; orange veins on a blue skin.
The water murmurs.
The pendulum of the earth goes astray.
The North Pole disappears.
The icy castle of wisdom and thought melts before my eyes.
The earth becomes a heated humongous ball, carried by Atlas on
his mythical shoulder.
Did you say you love me?
Flamenco dancers toss in my dreams.

Forgotten in the Port of Naples

this summer
meet me in the Port of Naples
in humid nights inside the Palace of Capodimonte
let's write again the "Human Comedy"
your love for me
a million of daggers
will cut the arteries of the blue sea
my luscious lips buried in blood and dust from the volcano
erotically settled in your poetry
against the coolness of the walls
your fingers, tracers of old tears
will mold us into a single body of loneliness and lust
sick with jealousy and shocked
a pale Campanian sunrise
whose rays, for centuries, barely can see
will find us walking hand in hand
along the quay…

forgotten in the Port of Naples
the memory of you and me

Sunday

this Sunday
hangs black drapes on all my windows
look, I packed some memories for her
my crocheted dress
he liked so much
the smell of jasmine from my hair
a symphony
three roses and aromas of some fruit
prayers and a poem that I wrote
the red of tamarillos from the Spanish bowl
the innocence I cherished
when I was sixteen
Lord!
this Sunday doesn't stop
she wants my soul

Greek Summer

summer
winds play on my dress
rhythms of the sirtakis dance
petals of white roses float over the bluest sea
lassitude spreads rosy fever
among the sailors on the ships

in the port
inside the blue tavern
we eat keftedes
and drink coffee boiled into a copper briki
feathers of white drapes cover my body
a yellow melon bursts in seven pieces
oh, its sweet pudicity
its enigmatic jealousy!
your hands encircled on my hips
the bluish purple of an hyacinth
whispers words of night in Greek
and by the "condo of the virgin"
we loved each other feverishly
for an entire week

Fears of death

fears of death
strangled in the heat of our palms
our bodies scratched by silver bracelets
glide onto passion's desperation curve
go beyond the locus of the flesh
kill our caricatures which people call reality
light ferocious fires on the altar of the gods
in rituals we burn to ashes our fears
dry in the smell of lilac
our tears

ah, I forgot to tell you when I meet you in my dreams
Arabella still sells bracelets in the silver market
she asks me every time about you
while lizards run their greens into the nearby parkette
I lie and promise her you'll come next time
to buy another bracelet and some juicy limes

now in the silence of long purple nights
the silver bracelets do not hurt my flesh at all
but every minute you are not with me
cuts yet another wound
into my soul

Before you leave me

before you leave
do not forget to take with you
our rhymes of love
flip-flopping fish on foyers' marble
the velvety récamier red sofa
on which the two of us inscribed
the decadence of our southern afternoons
the crystal glasses
now obliterated by the taste of the old wine
the plumage of dipper birds
submerged under the waters by our ardent nights
the blue imprints of fingers on the walls
oh, the withered roses?
you can have them
and with them
our entire past

The ridicule of the unknown

your eyes, the prohibition of cold winters
my eyes, the wanderers of earth
a copper sea mimics the candor
silence flies over the same archipelago
ah, Madeira
golden feathers are your waters
your lips taste wine
your breath smells corolla of flowers
we killed into your sands
the ridicule of the unknown
and went beyond
the ecstasies pantomimed
inside of the forever known

a golden yolk suspends itself in the warm air
a key is turning in a lock
the cries of winds vibrate an air sock

The Cello

I play the cello in the old streets
walls open wounds inflicted long ago
imaginary lovers contort in the air
and on my bow the grief of others
settles

I swallow tears and I play
the pain of those who cannot walk the streets
immersed in ecstasy and solitude
with all my sufferings
the walls I greet
till you'll come out
and you'll throw
a petty dime
right at my feet

Come with me to the Mediterranean

come with me to the Mediterranean
the highway of ancient world
for in the silence of its eye
still lives the infinite of number Pi

climb with me the Mount Parnassus
in fall when Dionysus' priestess will arrive
souls immersed in subterranean desires
into the burgundy of wine, let's dive

the bed unmade
your eyes still hungry
poetry is screaming to be read
come with me to the Mediterranean
where Pegasus is waiting to be wed

When Roses Sleep

open the window
let me feel the wind which blew
when I was born
open you palms
let me eat the fruits of the soil
which fed me first
open your heart
and let me breathe the poetry
of the sunsets when roses sleep
and church bells toll
over the land
where

I was born

Book of poetry

a book of poetry falls onto my lap
sinful kisses drown into the river's night
love equations chant behind the door
Beatrice commits the mortal sin
birds are nesting in my palms

the flesh of shadows waltzes on the roofs
a squeaky door stops wailing in the wind
imaginary fairies land onto your skin
my fingers knead desires in a dough
a button drops into a bewitched well

I bite my lips
I laugh
possibilities
range of poetry

Shooting stars

why would you come?
what do you think you can do here?
dark shadows battle in the mirrors
the walls are red
the laughter's a bright yellow
wax candles waltz into my tears
a silver coin rotates on my dark table
the Spanish chest is filled with photographs
there is no room on my bookshelves
for other loves

wait,
come,
bring the sweetness of kisses stolen in dark alleys
the snow in ghastly cemeteries is too high
the spleen of those who've never known what love is
(souls fly the sky when children play with kites)
the gnostic knowledge of the ones who died
your poems breathing solitude and myrrh
the untranslated birth of shooting stars

I see the stars
are you already here?

The Gypsy Girl

there was a field of poppies
maybe a meadow of cherries
or maybe it happened right by the sea
mama was pregnant
thrills of house sparrows
rested on her heavy breasts
moons and stars around her waist
and nobody heard
what the gypsy girl said
her voice was soft
her lips
strawberry taste
winds playfully ruffled her shiny dress
and mama left
believing I would be born under the brightest star
I would conquer worlds from near and afar
yet the gypsy girl miscalculated by one grade
and fated me to love you till the end

Who are you?

who are you?
which gale winds have blown you here?
which fallen saint showed you the way?
besieged by you, old loves abandoned in dark cemeteries
lament like choirs in my Hellenistic Greece
virgin thighs ferment inside your blood
scared azaleas tremble on my pillows
step in my room
and know no fear
unravel poems from your battered heart
scent the roses with my fantasies
weave lies into the brocade of my sofas
make those satyrs with horse ears to shut up

let's dwell in silence for a minute…
then tell me how you landed here
and who are you
my darling sonneteer?

I miss you

I miss you
like a little poor child
misses his home destroyed by war
like giant wounded albatrosses
miss their flights above blue oceans
like thirsty Bedouins miss water
like ancient swords miss their masters
like in the days before the resurrection
his followers missed Him
I miss your eyes
I've never seen

Profuse desires

rolling like waves on white marble sands
roaring like tigers looking for prey
howling like winds in gray towns of ghosts
resting on sofas like courtesans
praying like nuns married to Christ
tormenting my dreams
your raspy deep voice
dying for love

Don't wait for me

don't wait for me
go find another lover
I'm riding camels with the Bedouins
I'll enter Alexandria by morning
the day Mark Anthony committed suicide

don't wait for me
go find another lover
I'm in the *Île de la Cité* on Friday the thirteenth
the Friday which forever will be feared
the smell of burning flesh is choking me
the Knights Templar are shedding tears

don't look for me
until I'm writing you again
past sunsets murmur in gray fumes
and in the night before His resurrection
like Mary Magdalene
I'm looking for a tomb

Passions

I seek you
like roots seek water
the thirst which blasts within the rhythms of castanets
in Andalusia of the flamenco dancers dressed in red
I see you
the face of the lost stranger
dissimulating grief in autumn shadows
killed by the aurora borealis in the southern hemisphere
I feel you
dreams of wild young tigers
ravaging the flesh of prey with their teeth
in the Sahara of my burning suns the fate plays games
I chase you
the hands of nightly ghosts insinuate onto my skin
I drag you
into the lands of spells which crawl
passions strike
till all is left from us
are ashes in a bowl

Without you

kisses choke
sarcastic laughter
impregnates the air
a lonely silky stocking
falls in lassitude
dreams are blue
this autumn comes
without you

I want to die alone

I want to die alone
on a dark pebble shore
a thousand frantic seagulls
will sing my mass
seahorses
(my gravediggers)
will exult
the gravity of nonexistent stars
will bury me
into the scents of salt and fruit
and when my fearless Spanish angel
takes me to the altar of the moon
I will forget the misery I've lived
and never be reborn

Roots

drink with me the wine in Cana Galilee
my hair will wipe your feet
my lips will sew your wounds
a fish turns in my dreams
the moon has creamed her face
the world is full of clutter
and I'm growing roots
inside the miracle of water

I want my body burned

I want my body burned on pyre
a Viking boat will take me far on the cold sea
I want to leave my grave goods for the poor
and take the pain which branded their souls
into a bursting aurora borealis fire
I want to feel the sobs of the North Pole.

I want to burn inside the rhythms of the flamenco
flame in the dancers' passion in the streets of old Córdoba
I want to entertain rich masters for a piece of bread
inside the silent cries of those who are misunderstood
I want the desperation of the dancers dressed in red.

and you, the one who always claimed to know
what powers lie inside the jungle of my soul
you'll fade into your own acoustic lamentations
the fated day when I, the queen of sufferers, proclaim
that in the sanctity of the mandala

I want to disappear without a name.

I need you

lightning strikes the forest
screams zigzag in the air
vultures try to scoop my eyes
I fight back
the screams deafen me
bare branches scratch my skin
I gasp for air
a tornado rips my heart apart
my palms push back an angry sky
where are you?

Adam's sin

a canary sings
nuptial interludes
your flesh pays its tribute to some other lovers
transitory birds
come and go like seasons
noisy V-shaped flocks
I sigh
then I listen to a monk who reads
from a book of psalms
rings sleep on my fingers
arabesque designs shiver on my skin
pastel sunsets whisper in the winter's sheen

I walk through your dreams
soaked in poetry, baptized by your verses
your heart adorns my chest
(work of ancient minters)
your lips burn my rings, and with them my fingers
agonizing wings toll bells in the air
I go for your veins, my hands rip your shirt
everything's a dream
at the edge of silence
mirrors sleep and grin

you're forever mine!
do you think I joke?
wait!
here's the silver coin which can get you off

ah,
that's what I thought
you would never take it
in the lovers' bed monasticism's asleep
a cat purrs on my thigh
your eyes become my eyes
my skin tastes like sweet pie
see, why Adam was so keen to sin?
for hidden in deep waters
You is always I
even in a dream

Poems translated in Italian

by Flavio Almerighi (English version included)

You love me / Tu mi ami

You love me

you love me
like dolphins love to swim in warm
and shallow waters
luscious humid silhouettes of the
aquatic world
your fingers touch my skin
like priests in darkness the new
testament
solemnly touch

you love me
says the royal palm tree in the
garden
which every morning waves to me
I lost my golden earrings and I
found them
among the crushed carnations
spread on our bed
the night in which Mendoza wine
fermented our destinies
into its scent

you know
I've never understood why you
love me
the Howard Miller mahogany
grandfather's clock has stopped
somewhere it's winter on the
mappemonde

Tu mi ami

tu mi ami
come i delfini amano nuotare in
acque calde e poco profonde
sagome umide e lussureggianti del
mondo acquatico
le tue dita toccano la mia pelle
come sacerdoti nell'oscurità il
nuovo testamento
solennemente tocchi

tu mi ami
dice la palma reale nel giardino
che ogni mattina mi saluta
ho perso i miei orecchini d'oro e li
ho trovati
tra i garofani schiacciati sparsi sul
nostro letto
la notte in cui il vino Mendoza ha
fermentato i nostri destini
nel suo profumo

sai
che non ho mai capito perché mi
ami
l'orologio del nonno di mogano
Howard Miller si è fermato
da qualche parte è inverno sul
mappamondo

lost paradises hide in silver
bracelets
why did you come?
and if you came
why did you leave?

paradisi perduti nascosti nei
braccialetti d'argento
perché sei venuto?
e se tu fossi venuto,
perché te ne sei andato?

Languor of love/ Languore

Languor of love

Clocks drip languor.
White drapes undulate in the
breeze of a faraway sea.
The fragrance of oranges blossoms
in my hair.
Mysteries of the blue waters exude
from your salty skin.
Moorish patterns engrave
themselves onto my thighs.
Teardrops scent the air.
Our afternoons: never born, never
allowed to die.
Love.

Languore

Gli orologi gocciolano languore.
Le tende bianche ondeggiano nella
brezza di un mare lontano.
La fragranza delle arance sboccia
nei miei capelli.
I misteri delle acque blu emanano
dalla tua pelle salata.
I disegni moreschi si incidono
sulle mie cosce.
Le lacrime profumano l'aria.
I nostri pomeriggi: mai nato, mai
permesso di morire.
Amore.

Atrocities/ Atrocità

Atrocities

it rains atrocities on fields of love
predatory nights, barbed wire
walls,
the silence of asphyxiated birds
funerals of human parts
the geopolitics of pain engulfs the
maps
revulsion,
eyes intoxicate the shadows in
your chambers of delight
I change the course
I walk on heated rocks
hurt, the sound of waves invades
my mind
I sail my boat into the hearts of
those who are misunderstood
pain, the first dimension, runs at
the speed of light
space, the nothingness between
your soul and mine,
mistress of the purple,
jacaranda hides its kisses inside the
metaphor of us
a lily cries
I feed a child
with grains that grow within my
palms
it rains the echoes of tomorrow
asphyxiated birds

Seduzione

piovono atrocità sui campi
dell'amore
predatori notturni, pareti di filo
spinato,
il silenzio degli uccelli asfittici
funerali di parti umane
la geopolitica del dolore inghiotte
le mappe
repulsione,
gli occhi inebriano le ombre nelle
tue stanze di gioia
Cambio rotta
Cammino su rocce riscaldate
ferita, il suono delle onde invade la
mia mente
Porto la mia barca nei cuori di
coloro che sono fraintesi
il dolore, la prima dimensione,
corre alla velocità della luce
spazio, il nulla tra la tua anima e la
mia,
amante del viola,
jacaranda nasconde i suoi baci
dentro la metafora di noi
un giglio piange
Nutro un bambino
con chicchi che crescono tra i miei
palmi
piovono gli echi di domani

barbed wire walls

uccelli asfittici
pareti di filo spinato

Seduction/ Seduzione

Seduction

Seduzione

the rhythm of castanets awakens
the moon
on opal rings your kisses spin
a cricket's hitting a crescendo
waves tattoo dark shadows on your
skin
sonority, you who vibrates the
souls
of those who haunt at night
the Port of Cartagena

I toss in smells of apricots and
plumes
the Hand of Fatima takes off my
veils
your forehead sinks into the sweat
of lovers
who sever their veins
oh, dream of the unknowns,
you, latency,
the sigh of blood which flows
in spring both mud and flowers
grow

didn't you know
that when you said I love you
you stepped on roads of fables and
folk tales?
you glued your heart onto a purple
sunset

il ritmo delle nacchere risveglia la
luna
sugli anelli opalini i tuoi baci
inebriano
un grillo colpisce con un crescendo
onde tatuano ombre scure sulla tua
pelle
sonorità, tu che vibri le anime
di coloro che infestano di notte il
porto di Cartagena

Lancio gli odori di albicocche e
pennacchi
la Mano di Fatima toglie i miei veli
la
tua fronte sprofonda nel sudore
degli amanti
che recidono le loro vene
oh, sogna l'ignoto,
tu, la latenza,
il sospiro di sangue che scorre
in primavera sia il fango che i fiori
crescono

non lo sapevi
che quando hai detto ti amo
hai calpestato strade di favole e
racconti popolari?
hai incollato il tuo cuore su un
tramonto viola

smells of lilac and of roses,	odori di lilla e di rose, passeggiate
impregnated strolls,	impregnate,
seduction,	seduzione,
it wasn't me	non ero io
it was you who stole his soul	che ti rubava l'anima

Initiation / iniziazione

<table>
<tr><td>

Initiation

</td><td>

Iniziazione

</td></tr>
<tr><td>

deification of the virgin nymph
within my palms
the flesh of violet sunsets flips like
fish on land
my eyes, inheritors of light
singular sinkholes punctuating a
low sky
your love, eternal summer with no
births or deaths
initiation
doors lock by themselves
into the secrets of that which will
be
the danger of me
deeper than the darkest sea

</td><td>

deificazione della ninfa vergine
tra i miei palmi
la carne di tramonti viola ribalta
come pesci sulla terra i
miei occhi, eredi di
singolari sprofondamenti di luce
che punteggiano un cielo basso.
il tuo amore, eterna estate senza
nascite o morti le porte di
iniziazione
si chiudono da sole
nei segreti di quello quale sarà
pericolo per me
più profondo del mare più oscuro

</td></tr>
</table>

Amor, amore, mon amour

amor, amore, mon amour

love strikes like the Mistral in
Saint-Tropez
winds, hallucinations of pianos,
decide to howl in D major
enigmas move inside the wombs
incubations murmur under the
phases of the moon
bewitched, allegories of love raise
odes to exasperated nudes
a prophet gazes at a virgin sybil
whose liquid eyes foretold our love
in gold
reflections, lava of our souls,
a mirror hangs itself onto the wall
in the red room
a phoenix rises
our bodies drown
into the liquid time of the
Mediterranean
amor, amore, mon amour
the splendid flesh of a gestating
poem
washes our singular and frenzied
souls

amor, amore, mon amour

amore colpisce come il maestrale
nei venti di Saint-Tropez,
allucinazioni di pianoforti
decidono di ululare in re,
enigmi maggiori muovono dentro
l'intimo:
mormorio, incubazioni sotto le fasi
della luna
stregate allegorie d'amore
sollevano ondine a nudi esasperati
un profeta guarda una vergine
sibilla
i cui occhi liquidi predissero il
nostro amore
nei riflessi dorati, lava delle nostre
anime,
uno specchio appeso al muro nella
stanza rossa
una fenice solleva
i nostri corpi affogati
nel tempo liquido del mediterraneo
amor, amore, mon amour
la splendida carne di un poema in
gestazione
lava le nostre anime singolari e
frenetiche

Other Writings:
Prose Poems and Flash Fiction

The blue city

An hour fell into the sea.

The waves spaced seconds. The seconds shifted the ceiling of time. They ate from the meandering road of Cyprus trees which used to end on the steps of a small cafe called La Catedral.

We walked.

Yet we couldn't find the cafe anymore. Perhaps the building – with its aromas of paella mixta and fruity red wine – trapped itself inside the crocheted web of yesterday's sunset.

The moon hummed "Let's fall in love in Spain..."

You said "Forever."

I said "No, Conquistador. I will die on the streets of Morocco's Blue City on the other side of the Mediterranean."

Your green eyes sunk into a dense silence.

The moon stopped humming.

Your kiss came out of the sea.

It was blue.

The days in which the sun dies

I lost my name. Yet what sense is it in looking for it? You knew I would do it. You knew I would come back to you: my feet burned, my eyes full of sand, my heart crushed like an empty can of coke, my hands voided like those of King Lear.

It was as easy as you said. One day the celebration of the tree of light would be over, and nobody would dress in black at funerals.

This is that day.

The day in which the sun – eyes bloodshot, rays pale like distant memories – dies in the rose and violet of the sea.

In the shadows of those streets

I lurked in the shadows of those streets the entire night: solitaries, madmen, prostitutes, somnambulists. After a while I couldn't distinguish among them.

My steps were meaningless. My senses were tranquilized by that vision of him scribbling his last letter to me under a pale winter moon. The child was probably happy, playing at his feet. It wasn't his child, but…

The beat of the streets became one with the unstoppable movements of his heart in my own chest. He left his love to me like some kind of inheritance.

Why retreat alone with the child on a remote island?

Afterall the city did not do more than compromise the least part of him: his ego.

Blood is dateless. The ego is not. Which part did he not understand?

Attention

I resurrected him.

It was a mischievous act meant to attract the attention of mortals.

Instead I attracted some demons determined to follow me. I locked them in the sockets of time.

I feed them through cracks which propagate at the speed of light.

Bleeding rays of dark suns and dust left from what used to be your affection for me.

Words left to dry like laundry in the wind.

Words chewing my soul like termites in wood.

My poetic rapport with myself is bad.

My alter ego hisses like a snake at every word I write.

What's the truth? I have no idea.

Any act meant to attract attention displaces the truth.

Art

He hunted for reasons upon which he could build his resolutions.

He hunted in the wrong place for art is not the space of reason, nor is a ratio of whole numbers.

Art is the space in which the profane lays so close to the divine that one would rather find room to breathe through the eye of a needle than to separate the two.

And so is love.

Tree of love

I fed my tree of love with water from my blood, dried lizards, and pieces of broken hearts.
My tree will bloom during the Banquet of the Moon.
The broken hearts? You see I had no choice.
I am the defender of love.
I do not trade in half measures.

Identity

Anything can be said about that city, but one can never say that it does not have a distinct identity.

During the humid autumn evenings, the city looks like a wounded being, nursing her own lacerations. On the sidewalks the smell of dust overpowers the stench of cigarettes, and alcohol coming from her tiny, obscure pubs.

Clandestine risings to power, luxury cars zipping by, casinos filled with shady characters, rats zig-zagging in the basements of old buildings. Plenty of frustrations running through the city's blood like thousands of white blood cells through the veins of an infected patient.

A sea of beggars at every street corner: amputated hands, deep lesions, wrinkled faces painted in the colors of dirt. Pain exposed in plain view like art objects in museums: the only difference being that pain is free; the entry in most museums is not.

In that city our story began: a story in which we created and destroyed loves, trusted and betrayed friendships, invented beauty only to eradicate it at the first sign of dawn.

We tried to satisfy our egos. We ended up satisfying the city's need to devour us.

Replied

"If I could suck the very image of you from each word you say and stick it in the clouds, I would do it."

I replied.

"Oh, how mesmerizing and desecrated the sky will look then. Yet, who could stop you?"

Water

It was too late. I was already thrown into my memories, chained to my past, tortured by its unbearable voices.

I ran toward the ocean. I jumped. The water glued my dress to my body, hit my burning face, wiped my century-old tears. In the dark I went deeper and deeper looking for the bottom.

Few seconds, and I felt Miguel's body wrapping around mine. His arms were pulling me up.

My lungs were burning. I started coughing.

Miguel whispered: "It never happened, Clara. It never happened."

And yet something terrible must have happened before Jacques left Paris, something that was deeply buried in my memory, something that I was refusing to acknowledge. Did Jacques come to see me that night? Did he?

A horrifying thought crossed my mind.

Miguel, Angelo, and I would not be put in different heavens or hells. We were going to the same place, so we could continue obsessing over and over about Jacques' imagined love for me and that dreadful fated night that changed our lives forever.

That's right: a night that I couldn't remember.

Keep my memory

"I want your flesh to keep my memory, and your soul to forget me."

"Well, Angelo, crucify me. I said that because at the time I did not believe flesh has any memory. Now, I do not know what to believe anymore."

Every night the wounded blue of his eyes haunts me.
What have I done?

Shadowboxing

Glass of tequila in his hand, white shirt half open on his chest, raillery in his powerful voice, Jacques' eyes pierced into Miquel's.

'Salud Conquistador.'

Miguel laughed, handsome as sin, wind in his inky hair, flames in his green eyes.

'A votre santé, mon Maréchal de France.'

His laughter resonated in the depths of the night. A shrill echo came back through the cool air.

Jacques' blue eyes fixed into mine. My eyes flickered in his. He spoke.

"Sin takes place in the mind not in the flesh, Clara."

My hands pressed on Miguel's. Miguel's lips shivered.

Angelo turned toward Miriam and froze.

Knifes were out.

All bets were off.

One of us was going to break.

Attic Melancholy

In this attic there is no light anymore. Nothing penetrates the small windows from which we used to watch the moon's rays playing on the chestnut leaves during our first autumn.

In darkness I sit down and wrap a piece of a burned candle around loves which are born out of pity. How pathetic.

I hear a whisper: perhaps my old toys locked inside the old Spanish chest. They still talk among themselves, don't they?

You were right. I've never been what I appeared to be: a common girl walking in the streets and drinking mocktails in bars.

I used to laugh. Yet you did not drown in my laughter. You vanished inside my melancholy; inside the dead world to which I've always aspired. You've remained there forbidding my laughter for fear of not forgetting me.

Oh, that loyalty of yours in the mist of all temptations.

The night is blessed with darkness which makes way for light in the morning.

I am the night.

Nobody escapes me.

You knew it.

Sutures

"Oh, the four of you at that time!

Like the confluence of four deep, unsettled seas tied together into a magnificent enormous drape of spume; feelings suturing earth and sky like stitches suturing wounds; small fragments of fiction scribbled on paper; books of poetry resonating in the dark like cords of mandolins under the fingers of rejected lovers; fragile withered roses kept forever like relics in a church; the smell of fresh painted canvases mixed with that of salt water.

Any relation with the outside world severed.

That was the reality born out of your fantasy, Clara."

I was in tears

"Angelo, I know of no other reality but my fantasy."

Mistrust

I mistrust definitions. I believe only in that which hides behind them.

So did my father who built an empire founded on the unseen.

I am his daughter.

Sycophant

It rains letters of your name. The name of a sycophant.

Poisoned waters gave birth to a worm. What? Are you digging now at the foundation of my fortress? Your cherries taste like lead. Your flowers smell like rotten eggs.

The world does not speak your language, didn't you notice?

Who, him? Oh, he is my love. Too noble not to bestow upon me the right to fight you by myself. You will never be him.

I can strangle your infatuation, yet that would be too easy. Therefore, I'll let you sink into the sulphurous waters of your own envy until you can't breathe anymore. Eunuch at the gates of the harem – I mean that figuratively for I don't know it for a fact – raising odes to the Pasha and secretly hoping that one day…perhaps … you know what I mean.

You can't take down my fortress. My fortress speaks all languages and knows all sufferings. My fortress knows love. At the sunrise, we inscribe the tasks of the day on its walls. At the sunset, our tired arms rock our children. Our spiritual children. In my fortress blood is thin. Love is thick.

You are nothing but the poison of your sycophantic obsessions.

The world does not speak your language, didn't you notice?

You have no chance.

Tombs

The significance of that which is locked in tombs: bones, skin, my father's wedding band, jewelries, artifacts.

One hundred years from now – desecrating tombs – thieves will thrive on each piece of glitter they can find.

Yet the sole significance of a tomb is the love we bury inside it.

A tomb is a depository of physical treasures only for the blind.

Papá, I will always love you.

Ancestral night

The scales of the clouds gave me their blessings. Therefore, with my bare hands, I built my ship and I launched it into the sky.

Engine pumped by my blood. Sail hoisted by my soul. Deep inside the breath of the first ancestral night my eyes, hour glasses, measuring 30 seconds at the time.

The sky vanished. The axis mundi tilted.

I braved the galactic winds solely to find that thought of yours: your first thought when you set eyes upon me.

Lulled by the sighs of a suicidal piano, the time disappeared in another dimension.

The meaning of all things, never to be found only in one thing, spoke your thought:

"I want that woman to love me."

Like a somnambule, inverted upon herself, or perhaps like a soldier who forgot the purpose of her battle, I turned my ship around, and I navigated toward you.

The second ancestral night.

Love Battles

Rage darkened Miguel's green eyes. His blood was boiling. Bible in one hand, sword in the other, breathing heavily, determined not to let his Spanish Armada be sunk the second time.

Ha! And by whom? By a Frenchman?!

Wasn't Jacques supposed to spend his entire life alluring the other sex?

Oh, how wrong all of us were to judge Jacques like that!

And how dearly we were to pay for that juvenile judgement of ours.

Steely blue eyes, coat of arms engraved on his shield, Jacques was fighting to conquer only one heart: the heart of the woman who Miguel loved.

Both of them reduced me to a war trophy.

In the old, beautifully tiled hacienda, darkness broke loose.

Return

I would rather worship the silence of empty walls than your barren heart that you hold so dear; that heart that has never learned how to give.

You thrived in mud like a spring flower, yet by dawn you did not bloom. An infernal amalgam of erudition and sexuality eats your soul like worms eat dead plants. You became one of them: a decomposer par excellence.

I seek purification.

Therefore, forever forgotten – I hope – I return and kneel inside "The Wisdom of the Sands."*

In the distance patheticism licks your self-inflicted wounds.

*reference to Antoine de Saint-Exupery's *The Wisdom of the Sands*

Angelo

Angelo, are you telling me that last night instead of ending up in the room of your most beloved 18-year-old nun to indulge her virginity, so to speak, you ended up in a small decrepit chapel?"

He was furious. His voice was raspy; his dark curly hair disheveled; his shirt open. Nesting on his chest that gold cross of his which he never took off. I pulled the white sheet to my neck and retreated toward the head of the bed.

"Oh, no, Clara, I am telling you that somebody changed the room number that she gave me with another number."

"How?"

He raised his voice.

"Precisely the point. You did not ask 'why' you asked 'how'. You tell me how, Clara."

"Are you implying …"

Miguel entered the bedroom.

"What on earth…"

The whole scene must have looked ridiculous: Angelo in the middle of the room gesticulating, his eyes rotating in his head like those of a mad man or like those of a prophet – ah, that city in which the difference between mad men and prophets was blatantly blurred – and I, under the bed sheet, knees to my chin, trying not to laugh.

Thoughts

Thoughts: as long as they inhabit my mind, they are alive.
Yet too often they climb down on paper to meet their own death.
I guess I am responsible for that, am I not?

Bones

"This city lost its compass, I am telling you, Miguel. Bones. This city is filled with bones. Some alive, some dead, some on life support, some better looking than others. Even the sea looks ossified like an humongous bone condemned to carry the sky on its head forever and ever, amen. I am getting tired of so many aching bones. Articulations that don't work anymore. Well, apparently, some still crack, and then so many perforated veins in which the blood flows in the wrong direction. Truth be told only God knows what the right direction is anymore. And the cemeteries: there are so many cemeteries. And of course, that brings me back to bones. Even my blouse has the color of bones, and even the roses that Angelo brought me the other night looked suspiciously like bones. And look at the walls of this restaurant!"

The waiter interrupts me.

"Would señorita like some fish tonight?"

"Does it have any bones?"

Neither good nor bad

We were neither good nor bad. Those are words invented by us, poor biped beings, to chronicle our actions.

In retrospect, I think we resided in the unknown, in the fuzzy space situated at the core of that city: a city born from some kind of inexplicable cosmic irony.

Tragic

"His story was tragic.

Yet he was too shallow to live his own tragedy, and too weak to escape it.

It occurred to me that he has woven a web of lies in which he lived like a curious spider lacking his own body.

Night and day crawling, spastic legs weaving lies, suffocating anybody who dared to approach him. Empty, in the middle of his own cobweb, contorting his legs, existing somewhere between heaven and earth in a demotic world not created by God, but by a relapsed and dark demiurge.

...

Angelo, are you still listening to me?"

"Who dares not to, Clara?"

Self-sacrifice

The great poet was expelled from Florence.

Miguel expelled himself from himself to make room for me.

Self-sacrifice.

I melted into his being like an enormous orange sun into dark, desert sands.

Neither of us saw the eight bad omens of the conquest.

Our bodies were flaming mightily in the Aztec sky.

That inky night the fire of our flesh destroyed the temple of Huitzilopochtli.

What have we done?

Agonizing nights

A whole week.

Seven agonizing nights; seven suffocating nights rushing over me, parching my soul with their torrid breezes.

Myriads of mosquitoes murmuring in the dark, looking for prey: my own flesh, my own blood.

Nights extending their heavy tentacles over the city, strangling it as a venomous octopus; abandoning it at sunrise lacking vigor, emptied of hopes, filled with trash.

Glued to my heated body, lace and silk soaked in perspiration. I am looking out of the window. I can't see you.

In this city clocks have no hands, years have no months, months have no days. Outside of time, the city is innocent, perverse, philosophical, suicidal.

Shadows of your eyes; fragments of your voice hidden inside me.

Dark.

Flesh

Oh, that quarter of the city wounded by its own sexuality.

Every street filled with shadowy characters: hungry scavenger birds looking to devour each other's flesh.

Exposed skin and uttered sexual desires; bodies becoming their own souls' mortuaries; a type of grotesque Greek tragedy whose protagonists lacked the nobility heroism bestows upon us.

It was painful to imagine what kind of wounds could reduce a thousand of Petrarch's Lauras to infantile despondency.

And yet...

Soul Bonds

Winter night tormented by hauling winds. I lie in bed. I can hear that beautiful raspy voice of his:

"I have seen so much in my life: indescribable humiliations, deep scars on burned faces, dreams crushed like broken glass on empty floors.

We desperately want to love, to possess each other, caught in a perpetual rush to justify our existence.

Yet there is no love that can fully satisfy us. The passions of the flesh get exhausted in bed. What is left is exhausted by our imagination.

Physical love does not bind forever. Soul bonds do."

Memories of a silky African violet nightgown modeling my body.

Ah, where are you? Where are you now?

Destinies

Our destinies caught in the deep lines of my left palm.

With my right index finger, I trace those lines again and again, until I cannot breathe anymore, until my left palm bleeds.

None of us can be judged outside endless flights between continents, outside of our tears and of our love for art, outside of the slippery slope that runs from *amitié amoureuse* to deep impassioned love.

One day all of us will have to understand that the past should stay in the past. That day is inscribed in my left palm together with our pain, and our tendencies toward the kind of love that transcends any earthly boundaries.

Fires of the mind

First, one's mind catered to the other.

Then, they started praying upon each other's art: one's imagination crawling on and playing with the other's like two lion cubs frolicking on Africa's grasslands.

By the time physical love came into play, they were already burning like two pieces of glass in a Murano furnace.

In the end, a lonely man found a mound of shattered glass in a back alley.

It would have been much easier if they would have kept their art separate.

Yet they didn't.

The Chronicle of a Disaster Foretold

"Stop it, Angelo, stop it! What did you want me to do?

Wrap myself in the in French flag and sing *La Marseillaise*?

Write a book called 'The Chronicle of a Disaster Foretold' and let the entire world know that Jacques was going to fall in love with me?

I am telling you that no matter what things would have happened the way they happened!"

I was enraged: my lips cracked, my body tensed, my dress pinching my skin like I was attacked by an army of red ants.

Miguel entered the room.

For a moment his green eyes reflected incredulity. He looked at Angelo, eyebrows raised, his left index finger pointing toward me.

"Why is Clara standing in the middle of the table?"

Ah, Miguel and that dreamy quality of his voice always bringing back our nights of love.

Angelo tried to put a rebel lock of his black curly hair back in his ponytail.

I did not move. Miguel did not take his eyes from him.

I do not know how much time we stood like this.

Finally, Angelo spoke, his voice raspy like he was awakened from a dream.

"Oh, Clara? Clara is just being Clara."

I am the wounded healer who does not heal anymore

We were standing in the middle of the street.

The wind was blowing, cooling my skin, drying my lips, undoing my hair, unraveling my colored dress, melting away the earth tones of the afternoon air.

I looked at the buildings around us. They started deteriorating under our very eyes. They were growing older: channels entrenched into their facades; channels left by painful tears on wax faces.

Wet leaves caught in Miguel's hair; the old laurel wreath of dead heroes.

Miguel stared at me believing that my love would save him.

I stretched my left arm and touched his cracked lips.

I whispered:

"I am the wounded healer who does not heal anymore. I cannot save you. Go away, go to the end of this world, and wait for me there. Between two lives, between two centuries, between two sufferings, I'll look for you. I'll find you, and then I'll heal you. Now, I am just the wounded healer who does not heal anymore. He who touches me dies."

Tears were falling from his eyes.

Around us mounds of ocre humid sand.

No buildings were left.

Love in Venice

"Would you like to remain in Venice forever?"

He looks at me. His eyes green, his hair dark like the depths of the tropical forest in inky nights when the moon never shows.

I bite my lip.

"Oh, no, but someday I would love to live here for an entire winter."

"And what would you do?"

"I will walk every night in Piazza San Marco, at that very moment when the silence becomes so permeable that my steps can be heard from the moon. I will look for a new love in the heated, mysterious, thrilling nights of the carnival: changing mask after mask, dress after dress, smile after smile, pain after pain. Every morning I will mix secret essences of perfumes, seeking for the one that could revive the mystique of my body, intoxicate my soul, empower my mind. Every twilight I will dive in the coolness of the Adriatic Sea; my body shivering, my soul revived. In the night I will go to consult astrologer after astrologer in the less known quarters of the city."

I stop.

I look at him. His eyes engulfed by passion; his dark hair touched by a mellow breeze.

The sound of a church bell tears apart the moist air.

He whispers:

"Tonight there is party at the Doge's Palace. Would you like to come with me?"

"I am not going to parties anymore."

"Why not?"

"I died long time ago, by mistake. Now I am just a Venetian mask."

For a moment he looks flabbergasted.

His lips try to bite into mine. In a flash, I avoid them.

Marigolds

I run into the garden of my dreams. The sky opens, the marigolds yawn, and then change colors.

Silence. The silence of the night when my head rested on your shoulder; the night in which the North Pole caught fire melting like a piece of butter on a heated pan.

An African violet beats her eyelashes at me. A second then she shrinks into oblivion. Her memory floats on my retina.

Spanish moss lingers on the murky waters of the Bayou.

A purple honeycreeper starts singing.

Smell of fresh cocoa penetrates my nostrils.

Old wounds crawl on my skin; columns of ants looking for honeydew on a tropical tree.

I fight back.

Your eyes turn from black to blue as they always do in the heat of passion.

Wait... I am not with you anymore. Who is with you? Sheets of time undulate; lonely drapes in the ocean's breeze. I cannot see who is with you!

My breath accelerates.

I start running.

I hit a tree root.

Pain.

Millions of colors burst into my eyes; pieces of time flow over the forest.

The sky closes. Marigolds cry.

Where are you?

The purple lotus

I open my eyes.

Shimmers.

Over the night an enormous spider transformed the canopy of the bed into a cobweb made from white diamond dust.

I can see you through it.

You are by the lake.

My royal purple lotus floats silently on the surface of the water.

Morning dew adorns the grass.

In the music room the piano starts playing.

A bunny jumps on my bed. Is that one of your tricks?

Indelible memories of a night in which your hands touched my body come alive.

Silk embraced by skin.

You dive and swim toward the purple lotus.

One of your fingers touches its petals.

My pupils dilate.

No!

I didn't tell you. There is a love curse. He who touches the lotus...

I can't hear my voice anymore.

The music hits a crescendo.

The lake freezes.

It's over.

Through sheets of ice Merlin the Wizard smiles.

Maritime lovers

your arm rises from the middle of a colony of orange fish

a Portuguese man o'war stings my arteries

purple venom changes the color of my skin

the ocean holds you back

a red coral hurts my right thigh

my blood attracts sharks

I want to reach you

I dive deeper

phantoms of your love words spread on the surface of my brain

green ivy on a wall of bricks

seahorses show me the way

I see you

you swim with a yellow-edged lyretail

you turn around

your eyes pierce into mine

don't speak!

if you speak, we'll die!

wait!

your "I love you" cuts the ocean in two

silence

avalanches of water fall from the sky

stars shed tears on the forgotten tomb of maritime lovers

why couldn't you wait?

you smile

yellow angel fish surround us

humid silent touches

Made in the USA
Monee, IL
30 July 2020